THE QUICKSAND BOOK

TOMIE DE PAOLA

THE
QUICKSAND
BOOK

HOLIDAY HOUSE · NEW YORK

FOR "STEVEM"
& HIS GRANDMOTHER

Library of Congress Cataloging in Publication Data

De Paola, Thomas Anthony.
The quicksand book.

SUMMARY: Discusses the composition of quicksand
and rescue procedures.
1. Quicksand—Juvenile literature. [1. Quick-
sand] I. Title.
QE471.2.D46   552'.5   76–28762
ISBN 0-8234-0291-6
ISBN 0-8234-0532-X (pbk.)

FIRST OF ALL, QUICKSAND IS NOT A SPECIAL KIND OF SAND. IT IS PLAIN SAND. BUT WHEN WATER IS FORCED UPWARD THROUGH THE SAND, THE GRAINS ARE PUSHED APART AND THE SAND SWELLS. WHEN THIS HAPPENS, THE SAND IS NO LONGER FIRM AND CANNOT SUPPORT HEAVY WEIGHT. THAT IS WHY YOU ARE SINKING.

YOU SEE, WHEN YOU STRUGGLE YOU PUSH MORE
QUICKSAND OUT OF THE WAY AND SINK FASTER.
I'VE NOTICED THAT MOST PEOPLE, IF THEY
STAY CALM, ONLY SINK UP TO THEIR NECKS.
IF YOU HAD FALLEN ON YOUR BACK,
YOU COULD HAVE FLOATED ON TOP OF IT,
THE SAME WAY YOU CAN FLOAT ON THE
GREAT SALT LAKE OR THE DEAD SEA.
BUT IT'S A LITTLE LATE FOR THAT NOW.

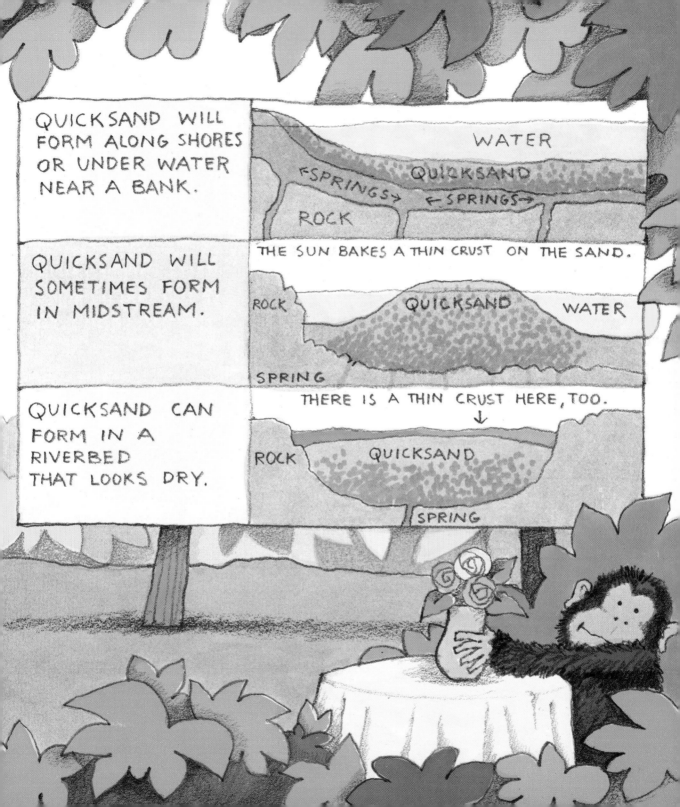

QUICKSAND WILL FORM ALONG SHORES OR UNDER WATER NEAR A BANK.

WATER

QUICKSAND

←SPRINGS→ ←SPRINGS→

ROCK

QUICKSAND WILL SOMETIMES FORM IN MIDSTREAM.

THE SUN BAKES A THIN CRUST ON THE SAND.

ROCK QUICKSAND WATER

SPRING

QUICKSAND CAN FORM IN A RIVERBED THAT LOOKS DRY.

THERE IS A THIN CRUST HERE, TOO.
↓

ROCK QUICKSAND

SPRING

① CALL FOR HELP.

② FALL ON YOUR BACK.

③ PUT STICK UNDER SHOULDERS WITH ARMS OUT TO SIDE.

④ PUSH STICK TO HIPS.

⑤ SLOWLY PULL LEGS OUT ONE AT A TIME.

⑥ DON'T TIRE YOURSELF OUT - TAKE RESTS BETWEEN MOVES.

⑦ USE THE STICK TO KEEP "FLOATING" ON QUICKSAND.

⑧ ROLL A LITTLE AT A TIME TO SOLID GROUND.

⑨ REST.

BUT, JUNGLE GIRL, THIS IS YOUR LUCKY DAY.
I'M HERE TO HELP YOU. I COULD
STRETCH OUT ON THAT LOG AND
PULL YOU OUT WITH MY HANDS.
THAT WOULD TAKE A LOT OF WORK.
INSTEAD, I SHALL USE A STRONG VINE.
SLIP THE VINE UNDER YOUR ARMS
AND HANG ON.

How To Make Your Own Quicksand

① MAKE A HOLE IN THE BOTTOM OF A PAIL.

② STICK A HOSE UP THROUGH THE HOLE AND MAKE IT WATERTIGHT.

③ FILL THE PAIL ¾ FULL WITH SAND.

④ PLACE A HEAVY OBJECT ON TOP OF THE SAND. THE OBJECT WILL STAY PUT.

⑤ TURN ON THE HOSE SO THAT A LITTLE WATER TRICKLES UP THROUGH THE SAND. THE SAND WILL SWELL AND GRAINS WILL PULL APART. WHEN THERE IS ENOUGH WATER TO MAKE THE SAND "QUICK", THE OBJECT WILL SINK.

⑥ TURN OFF THE WATER. THE SAND WILL SETTLE AND WATER WILL COME TO THE TOP. THE SAND CAN NOW HOLD ANOTHER HEAVY OBJECT. THIS IS BECAUSE THE WATER IS SQUEEZED TOWARD THE TOP, AND THE GRAINS OF SAND AREN'T PULLED APART AS MUCH.